the She Project

How *she* inspired
a community…

The She Project
How *she* inspired a community

Lauren Ohlgren

The She Project: How *she* inspired a community

Copyright © 2007 Lauren Ohlgren.

For information write Asher Simmons, Growing Art Press, 419 NW
16th Street, Corvallis, Oregon, 97330, United States of America

ISBN : 978-1-934367-49-0

Printed in China

Thank you

to the women of Corvallis, Oregon,

for their vulnerability, their stories,

and their willingness to play.

4

Foreward

When I play, the clutter in my life fades into the background. I am changed by the process of playing. The daily hurts are healed a bit. I revel in the moment, revive a little, become more engaged in life. I suspend disbelief and expectations about the results of my play. I am cften awed by the result.

I've known Lauren for about twelve years now. I've always been drawn to and impressed by her creativity. She has this ability to engage in a task without having expectations about the result, which opens a world of possibilities for her in every aspect of her life. Somehow, she enables this ability in the people around her, with the most wonderful and fascinating results.

The She Project is a perfect example of this. Lauren created a virtual sandbox and invited the women of the community to play. The result is truly amazing.

I learned of *The She Project* from Lauren as the first show was being hung. She probably spent two hours talking—nonstop—about the project, the participating women, the pieces that were returned. Her eyes glowed. Every story was chased out of her by the next one, filling every second of that two hours with words that elicited laughter and tears. I was hooked. I knew I would support the efforts to make *The She Project* a continuing event.

Asher Simmons

Introduction

I spent many of the dark and rainy evenings in the winter of 2005 with friends at the dinner table where we shared great food, wine, and laughter. We often spent hours in each other's company and talked about our own personal creativity and forms of expression. For me it was sketching; filling notebook after notebook with line drawings and sketches. Others had a passion for words, and writing was their favored medium. With the encouragement we found among friends, we decided to plan evenings in which we would come together to journal and to share the process of interplaying words with sketches, painting, and collage.

One evening I described two small etchings that I had recently bought from a gallery. The images were wistful, layered in meaning and open to interpretation. What struck me most about them though, were the titles. They were short phrases, partial thoughts, windows to the private feelings of a woman. The window was big enough to draw you in and small enough to leave you wanting more. Though the pieces were somewhat "dark," I found them endearing, and they also provoked a light-hearted, playful bantering among our gathering of friends. We imagined possible titles for art that we, ourselves, might create; 'She wondered if her butt looked big…' or 'She thought she had it together…' We were entertained and amused as we dreamed up more of these descriptions. We laughed at our absurdity, and as the conversation opened up and took on a life of its own, we began to see what we might really create.

This became *The She Project*.

In the following months, I gathered a group of women and together we designed the project, set guidelines, wrote pages of phrases to be used, and spread the idea simply by word of mouth. Women signed up via email and prepared for the event by buying an inexpensive 8" x 10" picture frame.

On the Friday before Mother's Day the phrases were randomly assigned to each woman and sent out.

We began with the idea of writing these titles or phrases into a party activity for a friend's upcoming birthday. It was something we could all share, a point of commonality.

The rules for the game were simple. We would write a list of phrases, beginning with the word "She…" and end them with words relating somehow to women. We would put all of the phrases into a hat. Each woman would take one phrase, which was to be the inspiration for the creation of a picture, drawing, or collage.

Although we never got around to playing the game at the birthday party, the idea struck a chord with me and I kept revisiting it in the following days. I decided to expand 'the game' to a larger community of women.

With a two hour time limit to create, they were to respond to the phrase—immediately, viscerally, spontaneously—with words, pictures, colors, textures—in any way that could be contained in the frame. Each framed piece was to be turned in the very next day.

The project wasn't meant to be about art. It was about the willingness to risk, to reflect on oneself, and to share the results of the experience with others. It was a celebration of living a woman's life. It was about stretching personal limitations. It was about spontaneity—the truth often surfaces long before

thought catches up. In that moment, life simply happens—without judgment or a predetermined outcome.

In all, over 100 women signed up, and 92 pieces were created and submitted. For the month of June 2005, our gallery was a local coffee shop, Sunnyside-Up Café, where a patient and supportive group of 15 volunteers helped hang the show. The brightly painted walls of the café were temporarily tiled end to end with the 8"x10" framed pieces. It was a remarkable display of thought and emotion, an intimate look at our community of women. In the show were the stories, hearts, and spirits of those who were willing to take a chance and embark on an adventure.

We held a reception so that all the women could meet each other and invited the public to share in the experience and to hear the women's stories. Some had pushed themselves beyond the intimidation they felt at the idea of "creating art." Others found it a novelty merely to have time to do something for themselves alone. Still others had strong reactions to their assigned phrase, wishing they had gotten a different one or wanting to change the one they received. Some women just played, unattached to the outcome, open to the process. I watched all of these women walk through their own gallery as they saw that others had put as much of themselves into their pieces as they had put into theirs. The project brought people together and I felt a sense of connection nurtured in that room.

After the show had come down, I went back to the women and asked them to share their experiences of *The She Project*. Some of their stories have been included with their pieces on the pages that follow.

I never imagined the impact this project would have on me personally. As an artist, I am used to taking certain risks, allowing my creativity to come from within, with openness and trust; whether others understand or relate to it or not. It's safe because

Thank you to the core group of women who helped design *The She Project* and convinced their friends to join in. Thank you to the women who showed up with open minds and tools in hand for the arduous task of hanging this show, maintaining it through the month, as well as taking it down. Also, thank you to all the women behind the scenes who helped in the multiple tasks that had to be dealt with, big and small. Deep appreciation to Growing Art Press for believing in my vision. Hugs to my brother for his support and for providing the spark for this book; my partner and my daughter who rescued my writing; and of course a deep bow to the participants themselves who were willing to come out and play.

Lauren Ohlgren

it's personal, it's mine. But to ask others- come and participate though you don't know the game; trust me even though we've never met; be vulnerable and show me how you feel, then allow me to share it with the public...well, that was truly a gift to me. I so appreciate the women of this community trusting me with such a private and personal part of themselves. Months after the project I found myself having conversations with women who still reflected on their phrase and talked about it among their friends. I love hearing their stories even now.

12

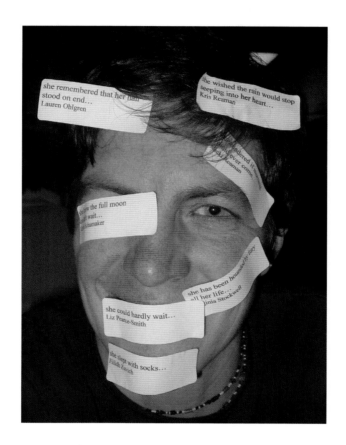

13

Growing up I was the kind of kid that followed the rules
to the letter. It didn't really occur to me to do otherwise
until I got older. In many ways I am a rule breaker now…
except when it comes to my artwork. I am a fairly precise
artist, having made silk screen prints for over 20 years. My
artwork is very controlled and clean. And now I teach art to
children and am constantly amazed at their fearlessness. I
even teach them to break rules… "a purple giraffe? Sure!" or
"what if you made that color go out of those lines?!" So I

She blew off the rules…

am trying to listen to myself and apply it to my work. This
piece was one that I did follow rules for in one way. I did it
in less than 2 hours… but my calligraphic self was ask-
ing for more control, so I brought out crayons and went
outside the lines.

Donna Jepsen Minyard

I'm a reporter, so staring at a blank white space isn't usually that intimidating. Every work day, I face a blank white computer screen waiting for me to fill it up with little black letters that are supposed to form some semblance of a coherent story.

Deadlines, even extremely tight deadlines, are also second nature to me. In fact, I've trained myself to work better under the looming visage of a ticking clock.

That's probably why I looked forward to the pressure of creating spontaneous art on an unknown topic. After all, every day I create stories that come as much from outside sources as they do from myself.

When I received my phrase "She has come undone," I immediately thought not of a woman breaking down emotionally, but of the elegant and slightly erotic deshabille of a woman who, in a moment of passion, has come undone. First I imagined hair falling from a tightly wound bun, but then the imagery of a loosened corset struck me.

Whatever I was going to create, I knew it had to combine imagery with words, which are my real passion, so I set about describing a passionate scene in words,

and using those words to form the back of my woman. Once done, I used scraps of a hot pink silk sari from India to form her bodice, which was seductively coming open to reveal more words forming her bare back.

Although the finished piece was not as tidy or as easy to read as I would have hoped, I was pleased that the concept matched the artwork fairly well, and that I wouldn't be completely humiliated to have my work up in public, the first public art showing I'd ever participated in. My name and work appears on the front page of the local paper on a regular basis, but having my artwork on display was a rather disconcerting experience.

She has come undone . . .

But in the end, as I dragged my boyfriend to the opening to see my work hanging on the wall with all those other wonderful *She Project* pieces, I was proud to have participated, and proud to be alongside a community of creative, passionate women who, like me, faced a deadline head-on and prevailed.

Theresa Hogue

She has come undone ... as the sun slowly lowers toward the horizon she can feel it soak into her bones, feel the slow, soft loosening of muscles as they finally protest their over use. Shifting under her clothes, her skin cries out for release, calm, rest, freedom from its bonds, silken and long, for touch, warmth, air, soft... She has come undone ... shoes slide off of weary feet, heels clattering as they hit the floor, stockings fall in a crumpled heap of web that is over stretched and loose. Slowly skin springs back to life as buttons pop free of their bonds and tucked in flesh shudders free. The ritual becomes frenzied as item after item rushes to join its sisters on the floor until finally the silken undergarments that looked so soft and wonderful that morning now feel like jailors, and they too are tossed aside until she is there, her self, nothing hidden or covered and she can stand there in her room like a new sprung deity, like Lilith, like Venus, like Hestia or Maeve, unashamed, in her celestial beauty, unbound by the trappings of her evening costume ... that at last what she is and what she appears are in perfect harmony, and as she stretches and pops and sways and shimmies and dances and leaps and spins and waves and hair falls in her eyes and belly heaves you can truly say that she has come undone

She wanted to be normal...

I'm grateful for the power of the women in this group and loved spending time in the embrace of the *She* Exhibit. While my own efforts felt non-artistic and restrained, I was inspired by the boldness and passion on display.

Anonymous

Illuminating my *She* phrase was simply fun. It was a light hearted and playful experience. I appreciate being part of this group art experience with so many creative women.

She changes all the rules...

Faye Cummins

She couldn't block out the barking dogs....

When I received my *She* phrase the images that came to me were of places I have been when I heard dogs barking in the night: Sierra Leone, Guatemala, Nepal and Mexico. From there my mind immediately shifted to my own "dogs" that also bark, whine, and nag…at 3 AM.

22

Gwen Spencer

She liked being self-absorbed...

24

Jane Megard

She liked being SELF absorbed

I was thinking in layers, with each layer bringing a new depth to feeling okay about a woman who is nothing more than who and what she is—with no apologies. To this end, I used multiple transparencies with images and quotes, over an acrylic washed background. This is a technique I've only begun to play with, and will be spending more time on in the future.

I have been more and more dismayed at how women are being forced—really the correct word is 'shamed'—into trying to look thin and young. At any time in history the 'ideal' shape for a woman has been distorted to some extent—this is not a new development. However, for the most part it has been possible to achieve the look by manipulating garments. Additionally, until the middle of the 20th century; being older than 16 really was a reasonable thing!

Thin, with the exception of the rare woman who has a genetic boost, cannot be achieved by manipulating garments, but requires manipulating the body, and often the mind, and certainly the basic habits of a human being. It often requires surgery. The measures taken must become more extreme as the woman ages, and a natural tendency to gain weight takes over. The extra weight a woman gains during and after menopause is designed for her protection. Without it some serious complications can take place.

Faux "Young" can only be done by subjecting a face to being cut and stitched. Mary Tyler Moore is a prime example: once a beautiful woman by any standards, her face has been pulled and stitched and cut until she looks like a caricature of herself. If only she could have been allowed to age with dignity and grace … if only.

In this country, at this time, there are far more middle aged and older women than young ones. We are not allowed to consider them (ourselves) beautiful or exciting or vital or even acceptable. Over 60% of us are 'obese' by modern standards (which have changed significantly in the last few decades.) We are to think of them (ourselves) as ugly, without self control, neurotic, even unhealthy—although very little real medical research supports this.

She is coming …

And so, my *She* picture shows a woman of a 'certain age'—a grandmother; with a body type that would be considered far from 'desirable' by popular standards—and yet, she's marvelous. She moves with freedom and is totally unself-conscious. Does this woman look unhealthy?

I hope that more of us can make art that celebrates who *She* really is.

Terry Weiss

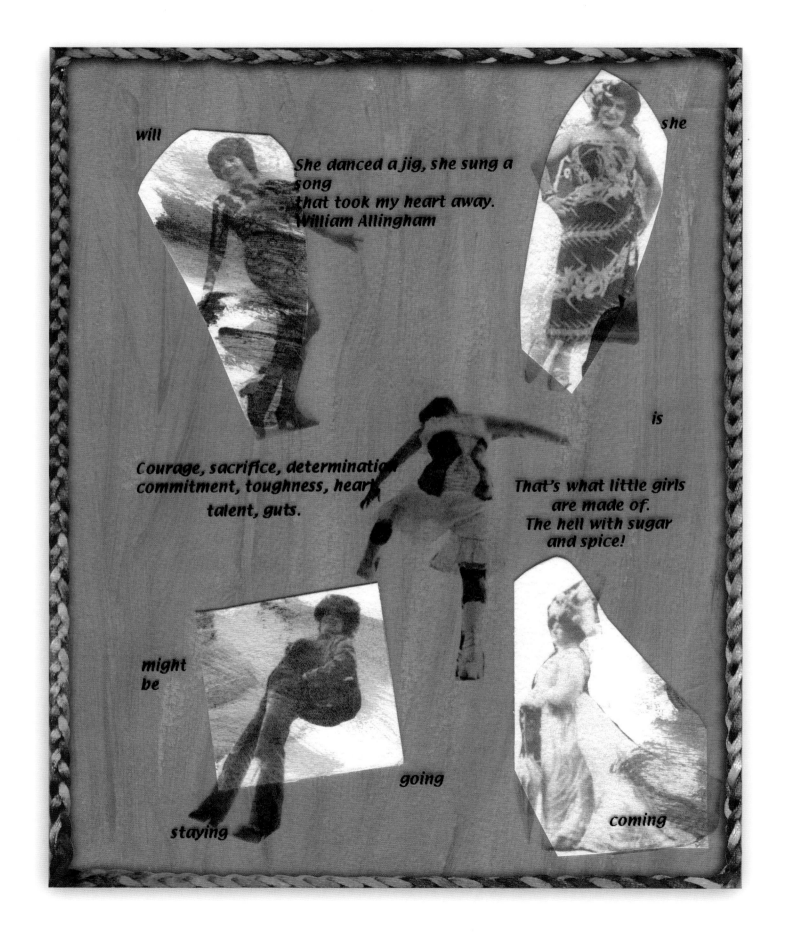

will

she

She danced a jig, she sung a song
that took my heart away.
William Allingham

is

Courage, sacrifice, determination
commitment, toughness, heart
talent, guts.

That's what little girls
are made of.
The hell with sugar
and spice!

might
be

going

staying

coming

She'd give her eye tooth...

"She'd give her eye tooth…
What did she have to lose?
Braces holler perfect scholar,
Smiling freely while doing wheelies."

Karla McAfee Williams

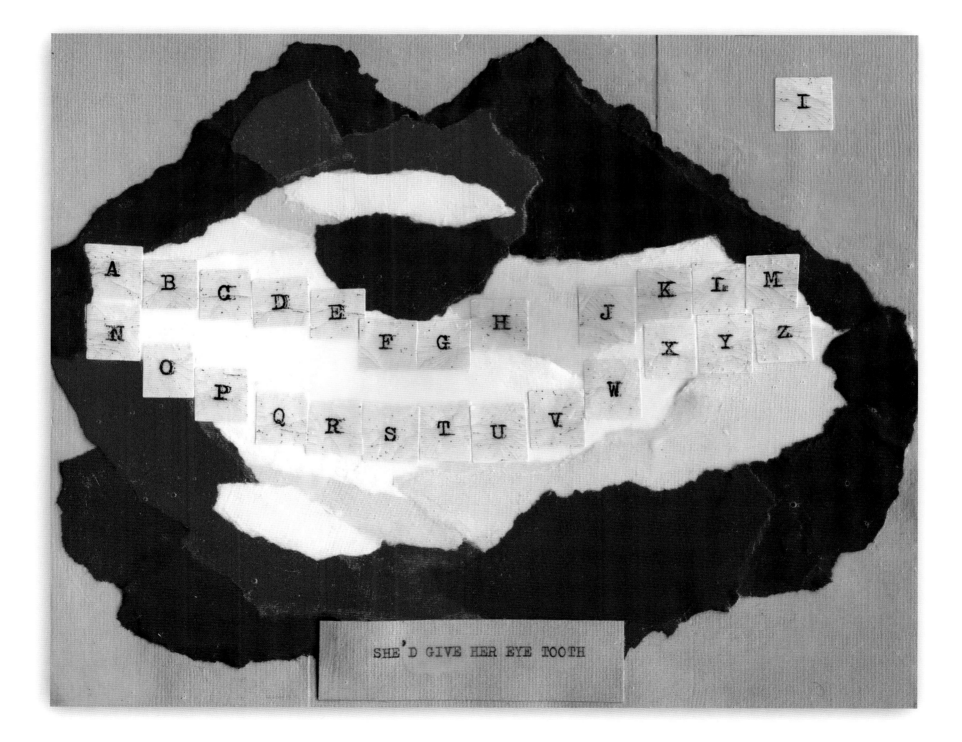

SHE'D GIVE HER EYE TOOTH

'She slept with socks.' What immediately came to mind was how appropriate this phrase was for me and it was obviously meant to be. Socks are a big deal in my house. My oldest son never takes his socks off, well except to shower and swim, and my youngest son and my twin girls, never keep their socks on, inevitably meaning that I can never find any of them. I only ever wear black socks, even at the gym, which people think is strange and my husband who is six feet five has really really large socks! I decided to draw my bed covered with a quilt made out of a pair of everyones' socks cut into little squares, since at the least opportunity every-one wants to pile on to mum and dad's bed to chat, bounce, shed socks, or fall off. My dear little daughter Merrin didn't get to be in the bed with us as we lost her shortly after she was born prematurely, so I took a little duck from the tiny socks we had in waiting for her and put it on the shelf above the bed, since she is still a big part of the picture. I worried and stared at my picture for a long time thinking it was too simplistic and not very sophisticated, but then I thought about the purpose of the project, to create what we saw, felt, experienced and then I got over it!

She slept with socks...

30

Eilidh Zuvich

I didn't get home till almost 9pm, so I said to myself that the first thing I grabbed out of my "collage box" would be what I started with. It was the girl on the beach. Then I looked at my statement and went to work, play. I simply let it flow without thoughts of what it should be, played with color, texture, lines, noting when I wanted to make it mean something and returning to my game. When it was finished, I noted it could have several meanings…she was so in love that "she wasn't paying attention," lost in her reverie on the beach; or, that "she wasn't paying attention," and HE was with someone else. And then, what is there to have her attention on other than the present moment?

She wasn't paying attention…

I laughed at the amazing appropriateness of the statements that the people I knew got. Somehow they captured something of us, whether past or present. I loved the adventure. Are we doing it again?

Sue Lyn Thomas

She wasn't paying attention...

TO PLACES   PEACEFUL. PRIVATE. PERFECT.

This piece is all about breaking the rules. I have pretty much been a rebel all of my life. Just ask the nuns at St. Jerome's and St. Joseph's academy, an all girl catholic high school. On more than one occasion, I snuck up to the off limits convent portion of the building to…"snoop". I had always wondered what was under those habits. I would roll down my skirt from its lofty thigh high position whenever called to the principal's office. And had I known what I know now…I would have broken more rules and done it all very differently.

tice pieces. I tried to have a plan because I wanted to be ahead of the game (breaking the rules) but what I created wasn't according to the plan (which I wasn't supposed to have) but it all turned out, just as if I had planned it all along. Dreamer that I am…

This piece started out with the whole phrase "When it didn't work…she pretended", but when I got to thinking about it, if no one knew that it didn't work but me, how would anybody know that it didn't work? So in the actual

When it didn't work, she pretended…

I had recently initiated a craft group that meets once a month. We are a group of talented artists and crafty women, willing to share our techniques and joys in art. A number of us chose to do our *She Project* together in the crafty garage. The whole experience was playful and social. Our craftroom/garage is packed full of estate sale kitsch and a zillion odds and ends. Everyone else was drawing and painting but I went straight to the drawers and started pulling out parts of old projects and prac-

artwork, the beginning of the statement, "When it didn't work" is covered up by the foil-cut embossed sun. (The perfect cover-up.) I go on to enhance the phrase with adding a "2" and "dream". So that the whole statement becomes, "(When it didn't work) She pretended 2 dream." Because, if you are a really good pretender… It always works!

Coleen Belise

she pretended.

She dodged disaster...

Three months into my pregnancy when working on *The She Project*, I found myself gravitating towards themes of body image, and the idea of trading self-control in for abundance. With that in mind—this fat, happy, circus girl and her sequined skirt were really calling my name. She looks quite pleased with herself… and not about to turn her back to the world.

Kari Davidson

she dodged disaster by being herself instead

And she couldn't remember why...

Marcia Chambers

I wanted to make my phrase as clear as possible for people (she couldn't absorb the message). So I created color that passed through the person, myself, but never really stayed there. At first it was difficult to create an image because I continued to ask myself questions like: what is this message that can't be absorbed… But that is the point.

She couldn't absorb the message…

Rachel J. Miller

She slept for hours;
then she knelt...

Diane Moody

Pray

she slept for hours; then she knelt.

Sleep

She was shadowed by drama...

Nena Bement

"She started to purr" these words conjured an image of myself humming along in my life, of everything easily falling into place, of this transition to a graceful, peaceful, creative, productive middle age. My interpretation of the phrase was an image of self satisfaction. There was nothing literal in the phrase for me, rather, the hum of creativity and joy.

A small group of friends shared a meal and then cleared the table to begin working. I watched my four friends being literal with their phrases. I got frustrated with my materials and the restrictions of an 8"x10" piece of paper. I am a dancer and a charm maker. Neither of those fit easily under a piece of glass. I glued found objects on my piece of paper. I collected locks of hair from each of the women's heads, green shrubbery from the yard, old beads and pieces of foam and I glued them all to the paper. I felt frustrated trying to collapse the heart of the phrase into two dimensions. I couldn't get the clip frame to fit over this found object collage that I didn't even like.

I got out my digital camera and took a picture of my creation thinking I could print it and then frame it. Although I was unhappy with my piece, there wasn't time to start over and I was done with that canvas, so I started taking pictures of the women I was working with. I took pictures of them in their act of creation. I took pictures of their hands, their faces, their art.

I got home and I downloaded all the images to my hard drive. I started to collage the images of these women purring over the photograph of my original work. Ahh, now "I started to purr." I was happy with my work now. My final piece included the hands of each of my women friends creating, a photograph of myself, my tatoo, a dance partner, and the found objects and charms of my original.

She started to purr...

It took more than the allotted 2 hours. The first two hours I was frustrated and busy trying to fit myself into my interpretation of someone else's vision of creativity. The second two hours I purred and worked with my own medium and my own definition of purr.

46

Lisa Esquivel Wells

She lost it...

Jenny Rettig

My picture's story is fairly simple. My phrase was "she turned to what fed her." I used some food items (lime and blueberry) to represent what feeds my soul. The lime represents my family's trips to the tropics—sun, warmth and immersion in another culture. The blueberry symbolizes my love of summer in the Willamette Valley—an abundance of natural wealth. The flowers have to do with personal growth and development. The photos are of my beloved daughters, Candice and Chloe, who truly feed my soul and sweeten each day. I did the project with my dear

She turned to things that fed her...

friends Cathy and Joe, and it was very fun to visit with them while playing with my art supplies. Several of the watercolor drawings were ones I did previously, where I was not satisfied with the entire drawing. I chose to cut out the parts I did like—to parallel my life goal of learning to value and recognize the positive parts of all of my experiences. Thank you for this opportunity!

Kelly Donegan

The She Project reminded me of the importance of friends. I was glad that I had been invited to join in the fun. I was thrilled to have an opportunity to share my creative self. I had to take the opportunity to make something colorful and beautiful that I could share with others. When I received my phrase, another feeling took precedence, however. I had a message to share, and I wasn't positive I could get the message across. I chose the completion of my phrase immediately when I read "She let her in." I wanted to share my thinking on the importance of confidants.

She let her in...

When I received my phrase, I was also thinking about individuals and their personal power. The story of "The Wizard of Oz" concludes when Glinda the Good Witch of the North tells Dorothy Gale that she has always had the power to go home.

Frances Beck

f. Beck 2005

She flossed as though she liked it...

Personally, I hate flossing, and avoid it whenever possible. So… what would it look like if someone loved it, and flossed as though it was something to celebrate? I painted while my 14 year old daughter and I relaxed after a busy week. I spend my week taking care of children while they play, and this was my turn. Many thanks for the encouragement and permission to create.

Lynn Kelly

"She flosses like she likes it"

Personally, I hate flossing, but this gal is clearly in touch with her inner dental-hygiene zealot.

Lynn Kelly 5/6/05

As a young woman, I lacked vision for my life. I joined in marriage to a nice man who could have vision for both of us. Of course, that didn't turn out too well given that my soul yearned to be able to sing my own song. Long story short, my *She Project* picture speaks to my desire to know and to live my soul's purpose. This "seekers path" lead me to study and practice shamanism. The feathers in my piece are from a Shadow-Self mask that I was able to release back to Spirit as I turned the energies of that part of my shadow from enemy to ally. It seemed right to save the feathers although at the time I didn't know their future purpose…

She never believed that it would go this far…

that is until I got my *She* phrase. They illustrate the path of my soul's journey as I live more authentically and with true purpose. Glitter on the picture speaks to sparks of life and awareness while the paper mosaic around the edge illustrates my multi-faceted and often challenging life process. I also underlined the words "She believed" because I, in my heart of hearts, always believed. And I still do.

Karin Magnuson

She never believed that it would go this far

She was so classy . . .

Sarah Graham

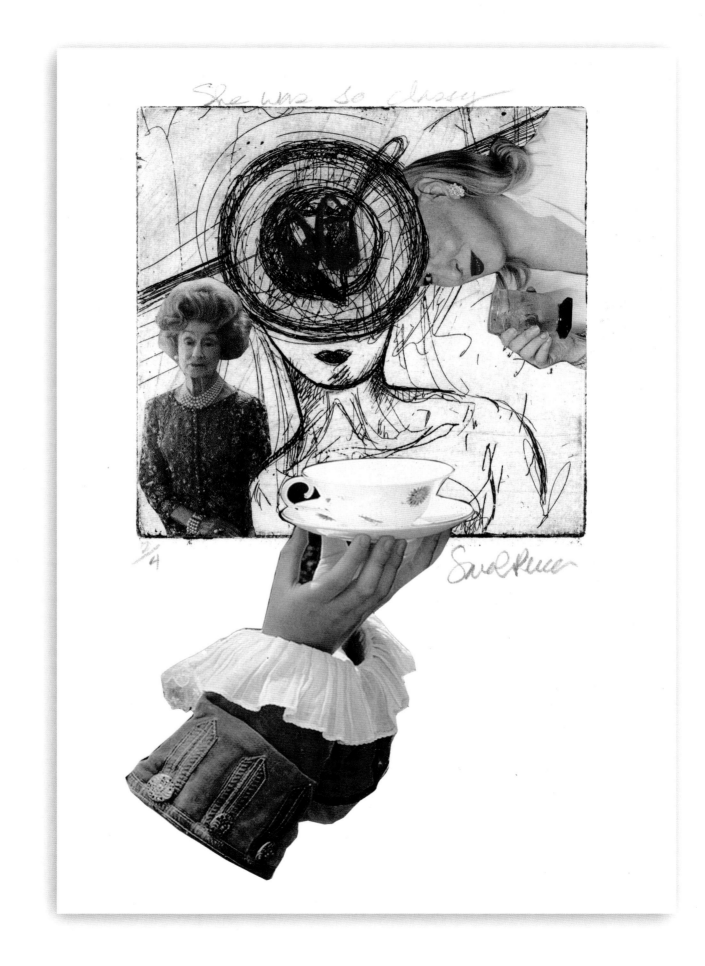

She stopped in her tracks...

Jennifer Lee Smith

She stopped in her tracks. Jennifer Smith

She was fed by things
that seemed wrong . . .

Kelly McGhehey

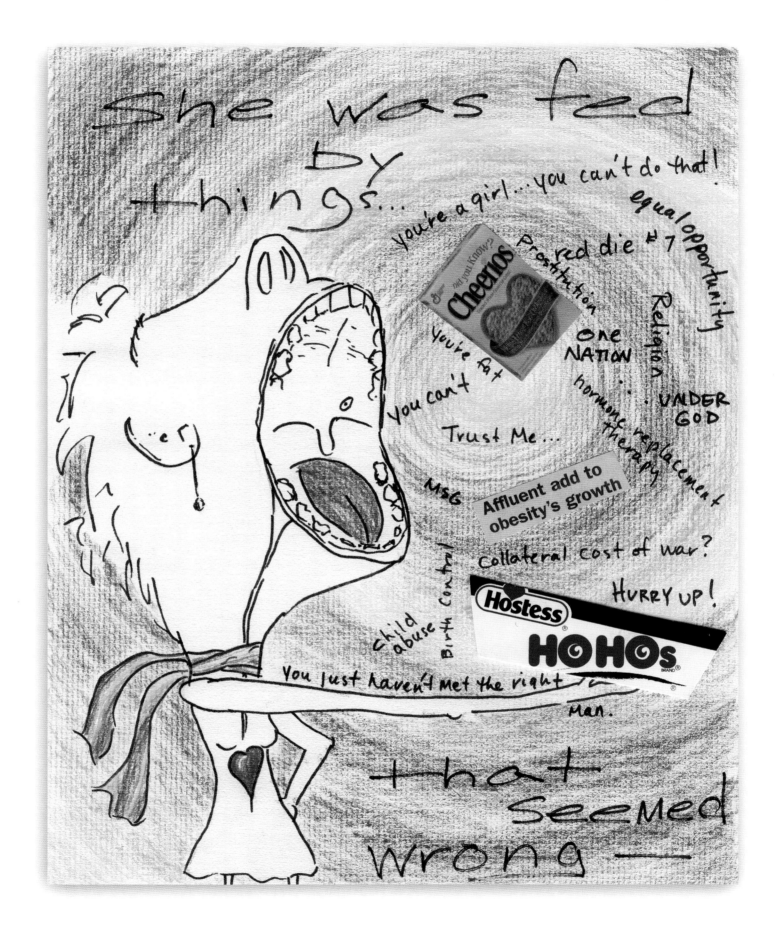

The day was full of anticipation for me as I awaited my phrase.

As three o'clock approached, I readied a pile of material to work with: some matboard that I'd already determined I'd do something to and a thin slab of clay to use as my "canvas." I passed the time cutting out some phrases from old magazines and papers that I'd accumulated from 28 years ago when I was on a Junior Year Abroad in Munich—a period of rich self and world discovery.

My phrase came to me at about 3:20 pm: "she got lost in the sun."

I started gluing phrases to the matboard that seemed to fit the mood I was in rather than the phrase, and then attacked the phrase. I had intended to do a drawing on the clay, but ended up liking the way the marks looked drawn through the clay onto the paper beneath it, so I tossed the clay and kept the paper. Then I partially obscured the quick line drawing with yellow and gold colored clay slips—the process itself as a nod to my *She* Phrase.

Then I got out a fat tipped stinky magic marker and scribbled. I love the fat uncontrolled lines they make. And love their toxic smells…

It was down and dirty, and completed in a very short time.

Something of note, I chose to do most all of the work at my dining table rather than my regular pottery studio. Hmm. Calling Dr. Freud… What is that all about?

Thanks for taking the time to involve us in this wonderful art project dream of yours. It was a much needed chance to drop into making something for fun and creativity's sake rather than all my usual reasons for heading to the studio.

She got lost in the sun…

Cynthia Spencer

Die gefährlichen Spiele mit Liebe, Macht und Tod

. Das Geheimnis der wilden

Was steckt dahinter?

Fernsehen macht dich

not invulnerable

She got lost in the sun

She had a funky way
of being present....

Meredith Sunshine

"she had a funky way _____ present"

She wished the rain would stop
seeping into her heart....

Kris Reaman

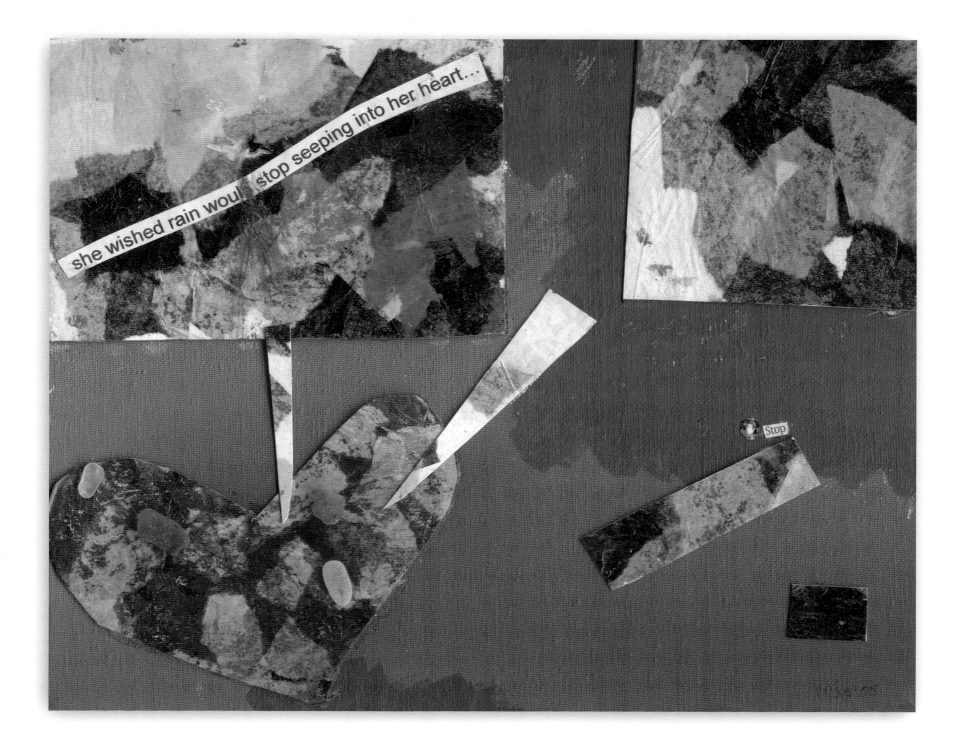

She realized she worked too much....

Cindy Cloyd

...Encompasses a multitude of friends in so many ways. Each friend has her way of making one feel comfortable. It's about friends that have passed away, too, and close friends. Lani, Mary, Lottie, Cathy, Myself, Lin, Kelly, Nanci, Judy, etc. More than anything its about recognizing that we are all the same—we are filled with the same stuff—only our experiences have made us appear to be different. Our souls are all enlightened and connected. This is so important to remember as we journey through our life, we are comfortable therefore all those around us are comfortable too. We are one.

She made everyone feel comfortable...

Debbie Maggiulli

She made everyone feel
comfortable....
her laughter was contageous
- as was her smile

With calming ease she brought
warmth and light into
the room

and knew each
persons heart

as if it was her own

She thought her forehead was too big ...

SHE thought her forehead was too big…

But really it was just full of brains and something to be proud of… In the end, she was so proud, that the appropriate title turned to:

HE thought her forehead was too big.

Which was a much more fun way to live.

74

Jillian Gregg

s from Dmanisi and
es mark new entries in
fossil record. Both are
uch smaller than a *Homo
apiens* skull. While Dmanisi
signals an early step in our
evolution, the tiny Flores
skull shows the power of
an isolated environment to
shape the human form.

1 m.y.a.

(s)he thought her forehead was too big

Africa
Homo sapiens
Approximately
200,000 years old

Flores
Homo floresiensis
Specimen LB1
18,000 years old

500,000   **Present**

Trees are beautiful beings, in every shape, size dimension…we embrace their unique qualities and see the beauty that they each encompass. Just as woman are… why can't we see ourselves the same? A glorified image of a tree; its roots and a dance that its soul is expressing… colors…dreams…curves…a perfection unique to itself. My body is a tree.

Yes, she smiled, these pants DO make my butt look big…

Simone Kujak

Several weeks before the official *She* day, a group of friends and I spent a pleasant afternoon eating and laughing and doing a "dry" run for the big event. We were given a sentence; we had our materials; we set our clock for two hours; and we began our Pre-*She* journey in ignorant bliss. We shared supplies, and tried new media and techniques; Mono printing, collage, watercolor. Soon, the room became very quiet. We were a little tense. We focused on our sentences and finishing our creation in the allotted time. Of course we all thought everyone else's piece was good, but secretly weren't so sure about our own.

Because of the Pre-*She* experience I decided that I would make my *She* creation using media that I was comfortable with. I prepared watercolor paper ahead of time. I thought of different weaving patterns. Most of all, I wondered what my sentence would be.

Then "She flew to the Moon" appeared on my computer! It was visual, and fun…and I had the ideal paper to use for it. I wove my piece. I liked the feel of my half dark and half light creation.

When I was done with my piece, I mentioned to a friend that I'd had two interesting moon experiences. I have seen two total lunar eclipses in completely different parts of the world; one in Cusco, Peru and the other on Whidbey Island. Both times I was in a creative environment and having fun with the people I was with. The eclipses added to the energy and camaraderie of both moments.

And then it dawned on me that I had WOVEN THE ECLIPSE!

Doesn't the mind work in strange and wondrous ways?

She flew to the moon. . .

Sally Ishikawa

She needs prompting . . .

C. J. Barclay

She flaps her wings
she flaps her wings
visions of women—flapping their wings

 a crazy idea pops in my head
my lips curl into a devilish grin
…
i know what has wings

for too long
that monthly reminder of womanhood
has been looked upon
as a sin at worst
and as a nuisance at best

it's spoken of in hushed tones
or in riddles
        she's on the rag
        she's riding the red tide
        she's getting a visit
        from her aunt flo
very few actually tell it like it is
…
i'm bleeding from my vagina

i can't do that
it wasn't in the cards

you might look at me and think
you lucky bitch
but don't ever be jealous of me
…

you would be thoroughly disgusted
if you had what I have down there

some say: when we die
        we die perfect
wouldn't that be cool
if it were true?

we could ride the tide one last time
into that endless summer
where bleeding becomes
a thing forgotten
…
except for me

to earn my wings
and fly with the rest
i would once experience
that reminder of womanhood
denied to me in life

i'd take that pad

look at it smugly

and say to myself
…
yeah.
i did that.

She flapped her wings…

Astrid Lydia Johannsen

The first thing this brought to mind since it is the most shocking and appalling thing in recent memory was of course 9/11. As I worked with the idea a little more I began leafing through a couple of old National Geographics …the words in the collage just emerged from those. Since they probably won't be legible in the picture they are as follows:

"America…a special place…what on earth does it mean…treated like a saint and despised like the worst sinner…winding a lonely course…Going our way?…the enigma…we were sitting ducks…blowing up the world…face-to-face with the past…caught in a shadowland between speculation and proof…death and destruction were the order of the day…"

This was one of those moments when I was just channeling. I wanted something that expressed violence, since that is, I believe, what is most often shocking and appalling (and unfortunately all too frequent) for most women. The violence in the world and the violence we can hold within ourselves. The skull image just presented itself. The pierced pennies (that was tricky—is that a federal crime?) are both from 2001 in keeping with the original motivation.

I find the image troubling still, which corresponds well to the driving idea of violence. In a world and a time when I'm trying to "be the change you want to see in the world." There is still rage within that must be addressed. Some of it is perhaps justifiable, some of it is most assuredly not…this to me represents them both.

She was shocked and appalled…

Joan Rose

Treated like a saint and despised like the worst sinner . . .

WINDING A LONELY COURSE

Going our way?

What on earth does it mean

A SPECIAL PLACE

The Enigma We were sitting ducks

Caught in a shadowland between speculation and proof

Death and destruction were the order of the day

Face-to-face With the Past

Blowing Up the World

My first thought when I got my phrase (I was at work at LBCC after teaching all day), "She couldn't find her keys" was "How lucky! She gets to stay home!" Women are so good at creating delicious private time. I didn't have anything set up with anyone, so I was on my own. I prepared to hole up at home to portray an image of a woman saved from having to GO OUT and DO THINGS because she couldn't find her keys. So my picture and my creation of it mirrored each other. Delicious private time at home.

While I drove to Corvallis to the craft store, I thought of a basic design, all the while, feeling quite smug that I was going to go home and do this ARTproject at the same time that so many other women in Corvallis were doing the same, about as close to a world prayer as I'll ever get. This feeling alone was worth the whole thing.

Ironically, my husband was hosting the monthly guys poker night at our house.

I dashed home in time to gather my supplies, my dinner, my wine glass, a couple favorite CD's (Diana Krall, Eva Cassidy), and shut myself into my beautiful room before the guys arrived.

My room was bathed in music as I spent a couple hours cutting words and images out of magazines and putting my collage together. It all went really fast and came together immediately. I was very inspired by the playfulness of the exercise, the mandate to be spontaneous, to enjoy, go quick, go with it, have fun. I did, and I thank you for the whole little adventure.

She couldn't find her keys...

Audrey Perkins

In preparation for *The She Project*, I played with acrylic paints a little bit on paper for water colors. I would never call myself an artist. In fact, I felt quite intimidated by the whole idea of painting something that others were going to see, with my name on it. Back in elementary school I was one of those kids who loved art class for the chance to do something engaging outside of the 3 R's. I remember time traveling way too fast and becoming so involved in my project that my breathing would change, and my world would shrink, and my cares would dissolve. So often, I would sit back and appreciate whatever it was I made and I would be pretty happy with my creation, only to look around and find that mine looked pretty sloppy, haphazard and incomplete compared to most everyone else's. I had let my creative experience fall victim to comparison with others. I completely lost the process part that was so enjoyable to me and more important than product. Art stayed on my list of things that I liked but came off of the list of things that I thought I could do. I put it away for many years until *The She Project* coaxed my artist self back out.

On the day of *She*, my partner, who is very artistically inclined, had organized a gathering of friends in our garage/craftroom, to sip wine and work on our *She* statements together. At the time I was struck by how well each *She* statement suited the personality of the receiver. My statement "She wondered if she could ignore…" came at a time when I was trying to decide how and when to try to fulfill a lifelong dream of singing jazz and which road would lead to this dream and at the same time try to maintain a relationship that was in itself "a dream come true." My problem was that I had too many musical opportunities to choose from and not a one was quite what I was looking for, so I was trying to hang onto all of them to see if one of them would lead me where I wanted to go. I was chasing this dream so hard that I was neglecting my "dream come true" and all of it had become shaky ground. At the time I thought I was going to have to put my dream of singing aside and ignore it so that I could keep the "dream come true." I also deep down knew, that if I tried to ignore what was in my heart, I would fail at both the music and the relationship. My *She* statement morphed into "She wondered if she could ignore…what was in her heart." It didn't necessarily help me solve my problem but it did allow me to express it in a way that I could see it more clearly and understand why it was so difficult.

She wondered if she could ignore…

Once again, I found myself totally immersed in my project. I forgot about my intimidation from all of the "real artists" in the room. My breathing changed, time passed, wine was sipped and colors played out of me like music. When I finished, I loved what I had created. I found that it was a complete expression of me and my inner conflict, right then. It was real, and it was hard, and it was right on. Before I could look at anyone else's creation, I claimed for my self a new title and exclaimed, "Ha-hah! I am an artist!"

Julie Williams

She wondered if she could ignore... What was in her HEART.

She dreamed...

One of the cats had left us another little "present..."

Rinee Merritt

She Dreamed...

She Dreamed...........
Of Tuna and fishes and birds (sometimes even little yellow finches) and dragonflies, and butterflies and catnip.....

But mostly Tuna

At first glance, I think readers are going to ask themselves, "Why would She write about a bunch of teen boys, when this was supposed to celebrate women?"

And so, to answer that question, which also popped into my own mind, I'll return to the "Surrounded and yet She floats" theme. I was surrounded by boys, and in that situation, I watched from a distance, and tried to feel what they were feeling, tried to learn something about these young men, something that might help me address my own anger.

What I learned is that men also know what She knows: That tribe is comfort. That tribe is support. That tribe forgives and absorbs our flaws. Although She would express this tribal acceptance differently—with hugs, with food, or with soothing words perhaps—He expresses it physically.

Even being surrounded, she floated . . .

The day I wrote about was the day before I received my phrase. On the day of the writing, I was all anger and stress and so I wrote about this moment because I saw teen boys coping with their anger in a physical way. I must admit, I still do not understand. And yet, I float.

Gail Oberst

Even being surrounded, she floated ….

Glint of steel in sun at the beginning of the 18th hole, as my son tees off. From the green end of the hole, I can barely see his group of the last high school seniors to come in from playing the tough Olalla Valley Golf course.

Mild Toledo sun, Pacific spring breeze. Five or six boys in matching striped polo shirts are playing mumblety peg on the green to pass the time until the final group comes in, the score is tallied, the places are awarded, the rank among the high school teams is established. I am out of place, the only girl/woman around, so I hang back, sitting in the shadows. Listening. One boy, tall and jolly, striped shirt, spreads his legs while the other, short and dark, takes aim at his teammate's pant cuff. The darker boy wipes his hands on his own striped shirt and picks up the small, bone-handled knife then throws it in that hand-over-wrist motion I know from playing this game a thousand afternoons with my brothers. Thunk. Sometimes the knife sticks, sometimes it flies and the boys go dancing to avoid the sharp edges. Goddamn, dude. Watch out. The are laughing and talking about college next year.

Aren't you Indian? Can't you get a free ride? The tall one sends the knife. Yeah I'm Indian, says the darker, shorter one, flinching, dancing. Chinook? Co-quell? Asks the tall one. Don't know, says the short one. My dad left my mom so I can't prove it. One night stand or something? Says the tall boy. I hate her, says the short one. Dude, that's cold. What's your dad's name, says the tall one. Richard or something, I don't know. How would I know, says the Indian. He throws the knife and there is silence. Not embarrassment, just some sort of shared seething agitation I do not understand. I am floating on this as the boys close in, looking at the knife stuck halfway between their tall and short teammate golfers. Richard-fucking-feather, offers one teammate, his voice tight. He picks up the knife and throws it at an empty can of Red Bull on the manicured green, the sport of culture a stage for violence. The can dents a little and knife bounces away. Another teammate picks up the knife. Richard-the-asshole take that, says the boy, blonde-haired, blue-eyed anger thrust at the Red Bull can, denting again, bouncing off. Richard shit head! Another teammate knifes the can, then, finding not enough damage done to it, kicks it and stomps on it, yelping, and now the Indian boy is laughing, kicking the can, throwing the knife hard at the can, his absent father smashed by his teammates, his tribe, his men.

Glint of steel clubs in the sun. Brown skin, white skin, matching striped polo shirts, cool Pacific breeze drifts just far enough inland to be soothing, spring cool but not cold. Halfway down the fairway, my son chunks his way down to me, dirt clods flying, comes in fourth; his team, second. His teammates, all in matching red shirts, clap him on the back, and they all make jokes about their mistakes. His tribe.

I am woman in the shadows, watching. Apart. Yesterday, on this mild Toledo day, I saw the way of men together, attacking their sorrows, and understood something new.

Gail Oberst

She wondered if morning would ever come . . .

Micki Reaman

she
would
come

ever

migrated

fled and

birds

micki 5/05

Thank you so much for all of your work on this project. I only got to enjoy a quick peek at all of the art but I was so inspired and touched in so many different ways. In addition to laughing out loud at times. I am a mother of three joyful children with a loving, dedicated husband. In the busyness that is my life, I rarely (if ever) take time to spontaneously be creative. Maybe distracting a 1 year old during a diaper change counts?!? Thank you for the opportunity and the wake up call to "be and act in the moment" more every day.

She plotted, planned, projected...

96

Candace Remcho

My phrase was "she found her heart's delight." The multi-colored melted crayon shavings I chose because art of this type normally causes me stress and is historically not fun—I have never felt competent to draw even a straight line—but this media (melted crayon shavings suggested by an artist friend) was fun to do and brought out a more light-hearted, playful experimentation that in turn made me laugh while I mucked around with it all! The items imbedded in the goo are representative of the things in my life that delight my heart: magic, dragons, music, the

She found her heart's delight...

love I have of life and the special people in it (including my partner), and the yellow fuzz is from my precious daughter's pony tail elastic—she delights my heart more often than I can count.

Elizabeth Wyatt

She laughed to herself . . .

I loved creating my piece knowing close to 100 other
Corvallis women were creating at the same time. I had a
couple of my friends over to work on our masterpieces
when we received our sayings. We had a great time! Then
viewing all the pieces on display, it was amazing to see
what others came up with. Although I haven't met everyone who participated, I feel I know them.

Cheryl Lohman

$12
Handpain*
Party Flu

COMPONIBILI

she laughed to herself...

I heard about *The She Project* three days before the final date. It was a busy week for me, but I was interested and decided I needed to do something for myself. I emailed my request for a *She*-phrase on Thursday. On Friday my husband and daughter were out of town and my son had a sleepover. Friday had been a full day of work and school, followed by errands and chauffeuring. Finally the house was quiet. I made myself some dinner and checked my e-mail. There waiting for me was my *She*-phrase, "The children clamored, she clamored louder." The story of my life. I have worked in a classroom either as a volunteer or as a paid job since my oldest son was in kindergarten. He is 19 now. My other two children are 15 and 12. I am now going back to school full time to become a teacher. I laughed quietly to myself and got started.

My piece started with some paper I had painted weeks before on a whim, but hadn't had time to do anything with. I enjoyed the process of tearing without thought and placing the pieces carefully on the collage. The drawings were done quickly without hesitation. They express how I feel when I am with children. I thoroughly enjoyed the process I went through creating my own *She*-piece. The spontaneity was just what I needed in my hectic life. It was a gift to myself.

The children clamored...
she clamored louder...

Lauren Chesley Whipple

She

an impetus to do art, and share it too.

I invited my friend.

We got our "phrases" and were ready. I brought illustrations from my recent poetry chapbook. Amidst her studio, tools and scraps, paper and fabric, she sat at her computer, and I settled in a comfortable chair, with sketchbook, pen, watercolor crayons. Concentration.

Years ago, I titled one poetry collection "she." Interesting, someone else with the same fascination with what the third-person could elicit about the personal.

My "free-write" filled the page; I followed my words around. "She lived out loud" took me back to Kindergarten naptime: RuthEllen and I on our little rugs, under a table, whispering. Abruptly I was dragged away. "No talking at naptime!" Then I wrote about embarrassment at having to stay after in first-grade; guilty of talking in class. Schooling meant being quieted. At home, my mother, hushing us from yelling with "What will the neighbors think?" Our daughter's report cards said, "excessive talking." The ongoing conflict: society's hushing of women vs. raising our own voices.

My writing wandered to being covered up, under covers, under shawls; my words then explored fabric, rags, household chores; *she* has been wrung out, hung up, rinsed, frayed, mended . . .. Associations were fast, loose. Fun.

After an hour, my friend and I paused; I looked at her Photoshop draft; she listened to me read. She was unsatisfied with one part of her image. I panicked: mine was still so rough, with no visuals .. .

More writing. Then a different phase: cutting words, choosing, arranging.
(once)
hushed, shshsh'd,
muffled and stifled
absorbed, soundproofed,
shut up, stilled
She
peeps out   pipes up
snaps open, blurts forth
living out
out-living
lives   out   loud

Some of my drawings fit. I scrunched Kleenex (as if from purses of my mother, aunts) into a backdrop of "clouds." Added bright red thread, running loudly through "her" life..

I ran outside, yanked poppy petals. Fertility, the instinct to express oneself even when we're covered over. Peeps out. Blurting forth. Aloud.

She lived out loud . . .

Almost quit. Then persevered.

Complete, framed, hung.

But just a draft.

I will go back to the rags-and wrung-out piece: a quilting friend will collaborate on fabric-and-words. And I'll get around to memoir pieces about being hushed.

A book of *She*—part of our whole story, the big picture.

Jana Zvibleman

(once)

hushed, shshsh'd,

muffled and stifled

absorbed, soundproofed,

shut·up, stilled

she

peeps out   pipes up

snaps open, blurts forth

out·living
living out

lives out loud

So, let's see…

First I didn't want to participate as I felt a little too much pressure (only two hours, what if I don't get a good idea?) but then I decided to do it anyway, thanks to Jennifer who kept on talking about it and finally persuading me to join her and her friends for that evening at her place.

I was pretty curious what my phrase would be, so I checked already in the afternoon (OK, I guess that was a little bit of cheating, as we met in the evening). That gave me some time to think about my phrase: She Giggled Softly…

I decided pretty quickly on the soft, warm colors I wanted to use, which I think fit the sentence. What's in the picture took more time to develop, although it was a thought I had early and then came back to. It's pretty hard to see, but actually the picture shows a woman, sitting with her head slightly bent back. She's holding a

glass of wine and her soft giggle fills the room. The reason for her soft giggling is not completely clear. It may be a comfortable conversation she's having or perhaps she's in a more intimate mood, who knows…

Well, that's pretty much it. I'm glad Jen convinced me to come as it was fun being together and being creative!

She giggles softly…

Heike Ocko

She looked back at her body . . .

Chris Barclay

SHE LOOKED BACK AT HER BODY

MAY 6, 2005 CHRIS BARCLAY

SHE STORMS

She looked back at her body, rocks
stacked in trailside cairns.
It has guided and clattered,
been the text
and context, been weathered.
But it is always
the weather.

She was about to leave...

Erin Ryan

The only thing I could think of at the time of *The She Project* creation is my girlfriend, Tracy, and how committed she is to the beauty of our lawn and garden. She inspired me to make this project out of dried flowers. She planted the flowers and they bloomed. I picked them and arranged them into the frame. I can't take credit for the whole thing: it was a joint effort between us. I didn't know if the flowers would hold their color and form, but I am amazed to see that 6 months later they still hold their color and form, just as Tracy and my relationship stays strong. That is the analogy I see in this project.

Tracy continues to keep my yard beautiful and I continue to see her as beautiful. Our relationship stays strong as we appreciate each other's talents. I am so thankful!

She and I are in love, dancing, touching . . .

Lucy Watts

She and I are in love,

Dancing, touching...

Did she starve in her body
as well as her heart...

Megan Houser

fibula

ed space
ticulation
fibula
es a
tion in
fibula and
iated
ors of
great toe.

during bipedal walking.

flexor hallucis
longus tendon

Did she starve in her body
as well as her heart...

She welcomed the light...

"She Welcomed the Light" signifies a radiance that
symbolizes the glory, splendor and joy of life.

Judith M. Sander

She welcomed the Light......

I had been looking forward to beginning *The She Project* since I had read about it in the paper. I blocked the Friday evening in my calendar and told my husband about it. The evening arrived and I took my glass of wine and enthusiasm down to the studio.

Only a few minutes into it, I reached a snag. My husband came down, wondering why I was taking this time for my artistic pursuits, when it was usually spent with him. It took about 10 minutes explaining how I had been looking forward to *The She Project,* what this project was about, and why I had allocated exactly this time to it. I almost backed out at the last minute because the confrontation did not seem to be worth it. Luckily, he grasped my intensity and backed down.

Now I was on edge. I had a limited amount of time, a disappointing confrontation to erase, and the clock had been ticking for about 15 minutes! I spent the next 45 minutes with my sketchbooks open, various materials and media scattered around me in the studio. I was panicked. The ideas had stalled because of my stressed state of mind. How was I to pull this off so quickly? What kind of quality was I going to establish? Was this the face that I wanted to show the world?

Finally, I took my small piece of paper, a seed of an idea and started to work. The stress melted away and I enjoyed the sense of the pigment flowing on the paper. I ripped hand painted tissue and news articles and adhered them to the surface. The spirit of the piece was flowing up through me. This was what it was all about. This was why I had been so excited about the project when I first grasped the concept. It did not matter how

She reached out to redirect the flow . . .

the final art work looked, what was needed was coming into fruition as long as I relaxed into it.

I finished the piece with 10 minutes to spare: to clean my brushes, to think of all the other *She* that were with me and to give my thanks.

Carolee S. Clark

She was quiet...

Joanne McLennan

SHE IS QUIET

She felt strong . . .

In the light of summer afternoons, she became strong and
healed. The light filtered down to her in the shade of her
aging pear tree. Grapes, blackberries, and red roses grew
along the branches just beyond her reach and she tasted
their fragrance. There was a buzz of bees, a squawk of jays,
and the silent passing of the violet swallows.

Caterina De Francesco

She fed me...

124

Laura A. South-Oryshchyn

She needs prompting...

My phrase was "She needs prompting . . ." and my immediate response was ". . . to walk away." The image of entanglement and attachments accompanied the words in my minds eye. I am drawn to situations where I am needed. It is terrain where I believe, as a woman, I am particularly at home. But of course it is not always healthy for me or those who "need" me. I often need prompting to walk away.

Susie Lisser

She needs prompting . . .

to walk away.

She lamented...

Tammy Myhrum

The term "global oil-production peak" means that most oil it will ever produce in a given year and usually represented graphically in a bell curve world's all-time total endowment, meaning s, but there's a big catch: It's the half that is poorer quality and located mostly in places ex

SHE

T ____ as ____ wn oil peak–about ha ____ y ____ it ran just above 5 co ____ ve se ____ e roughly 20 milli two-thirds of our oil, and the ratio will continue

The U.S. peak in 1970 brough roducers, chiefly OPEC, wer esponse, frantic developmen ssentially saved the West's a Meanwhile, worldwide d co

Some "cornucopian ____ will naturally re ____

____ ave b ____ n som ____ India ____ ot up, and ____ of g ____ sing up its pr ____ prec ____ tions and now

fossil-fuel ____ ythin

It will change every ____

To aggra ____ ____ frenet ____ ey ____ -pla ____ 97 ____ , th ____ ____ chan ____ e ro ____ plant b ____

LAMENTED

The ____ ____ s that we are entering a h ____ ____ entially great instab ____ ____ lence and hardship ____ ____ eopolitical maneuvering aro ____ d's ____ chest energy regions ____ ____ eady led to war and pro ____ ore international military conflict. ____ ____ ____ ____ eonta ____ ____ thirds of the world's remain ____ g oil supplies, the U.S. has attempted desper ____ ____ ____ , in effect, opening a big police station in Iraq. The intent was not just to secu ____ ____ fy and influence the behavior of neighboring states around the Persian Gulf, especiall ____ ____ ____ Arabia. The results ____ ave been far from entirely positive, and our future prospects in that pa ____ ____ world are not something ____ l altogether confident about.

Text From The Long Emergency: Howard Kunstler

She (Lauren) sat on the sofa in NYC discussing *The She Project* with Ann Curry of the Today Show…

She (Ann Curry) was fascinated…oh honey, she bought a book and was stoked to start her own group next year… she recommended it to all her friends for the holidays and the world as well…

She balanced on the fence…

As will many other *She* women who have yet to understand what they are capable of if only they will take a risk…and connect with other women within their communities!!!

Ella Rhoades

She moves her hand down my thigh...

Shannon Rettig

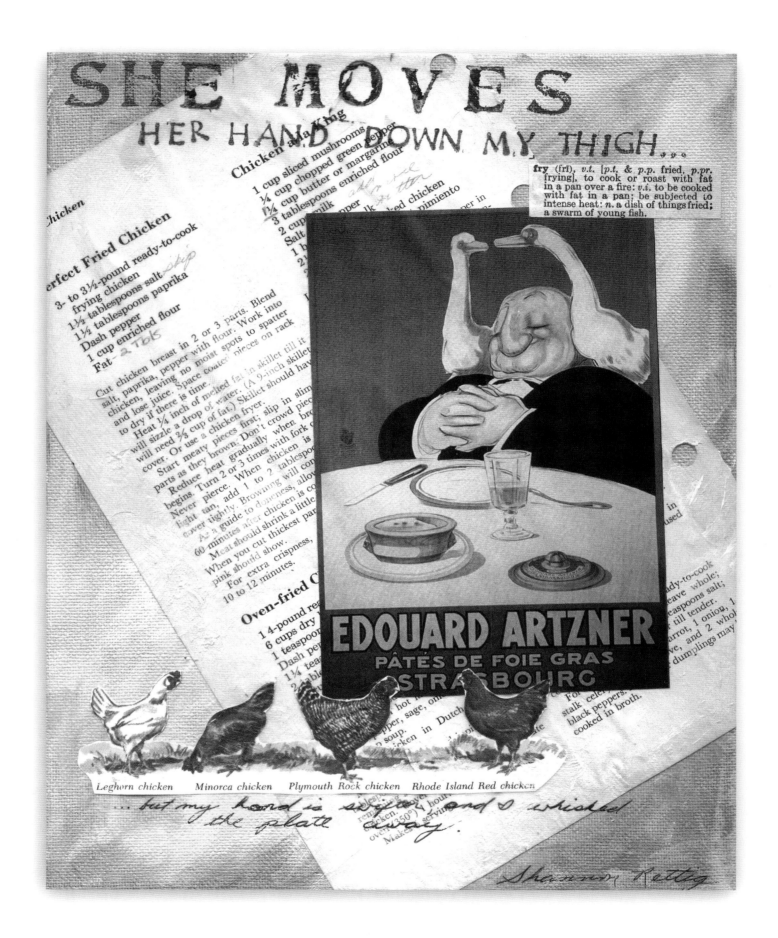

It takes me so long decide what to use.

On the table are paints, crayons, piles of colored paper, feathers, twine. There are charcoals and colcred pencils, magazines. How do I choose? How can I focus?

Thoughts of my son Zach are sticking in my head.

Things changed when he went to live with his dad, almost 4 years ago. I mailed birthday presents, a few letters, not too often, just enough to remind him I still exist. No answers.

She had a heart of gold.

What colors do I use? How can I possibly create right now?

Yesterday I heard through a near-stranger that Zach, now 17, is out of the house. Kicked out, she says. I spent the morning on the phone. I tracked down where he was staying, left a message.

Aching, I reach for a box of soft oil pastels.

I think of reds and orange, pain, ache.

A heart made pure by fire.

I could have fought for visits through the legal system. Was I crazy to let him go? I have always wanted him to have the freedom to decide when to see me.

But this missing him hurts like fire.

With a heavy hand, I begin to draw. The crayon skids across the paper…

She had a heart of gold…

Amy Crevola

When I first received my *She* phrase I was quite surprised by it and thought "What????—You've got to be kidding." I was expecting something a bit more empowering than "She noticed she had dirt under all of her fingernails." Naturally I became very resistant. I almost called my friend to see what ideas she could think of and then I simply decided to put my fear aside and "go for it!"

A few of the women from my Artist's Way group were gathering to work on our projects together. I had formulated an idea of what I wanted to create and the meaning it held for me and I ran out the door, goodies in tow. I had decided that the meaning the phrase held for me was one of duality; the loving things that women do which gets their nails dirty, and what we do to clean them. The idea that women give so much and then wake up one day and realize that we have not been taking care of ourselves.

As we spread ourselves over a table for four I realized that I had accidentally left behind the most important things that I had planned on using for my creation. The absence of these items made it necessary for me to attempt to find some like-items or formulate an entirely new idea. And so I spent two hours rifling through numerous magazines to find the "right" words and pictures that I wanted to use to express myself. Feeling very blocked I became more and more frustrated. As the others at the table finished with their own creations, they helped me look through magazines; but this process only served to frustrate me more, as it simply wasn't coming together and it just wasn't feeling authentic. By this time I had developed a massive headache and finally conceded defeat. And so, my headache and I headed home with our goodies in tow, holding the thought that I would awake in the morning with my original items, headache-less and inspired. That is exactly what happened.

The following morning, over a cup of coffee, I began snipping things here and there from the pages of several magazines, cutting out words, faces, and lots and lots and lots of hands. I colored dirt under some of the nails and painted the others with bright colored nail polish in hopes that they would reflect through the glass in the frame. As I worked, the project began creating itself and,

She noticed that she had dirt under all of her fingernails . . .

far from my "original idea," was surprisingly a lot of fun and very rewarding. How wonderful! Who would have thought—a little piece of "me" in an 8 x 10 frame.

Thank you for the fun!

Liz Dieckhoff

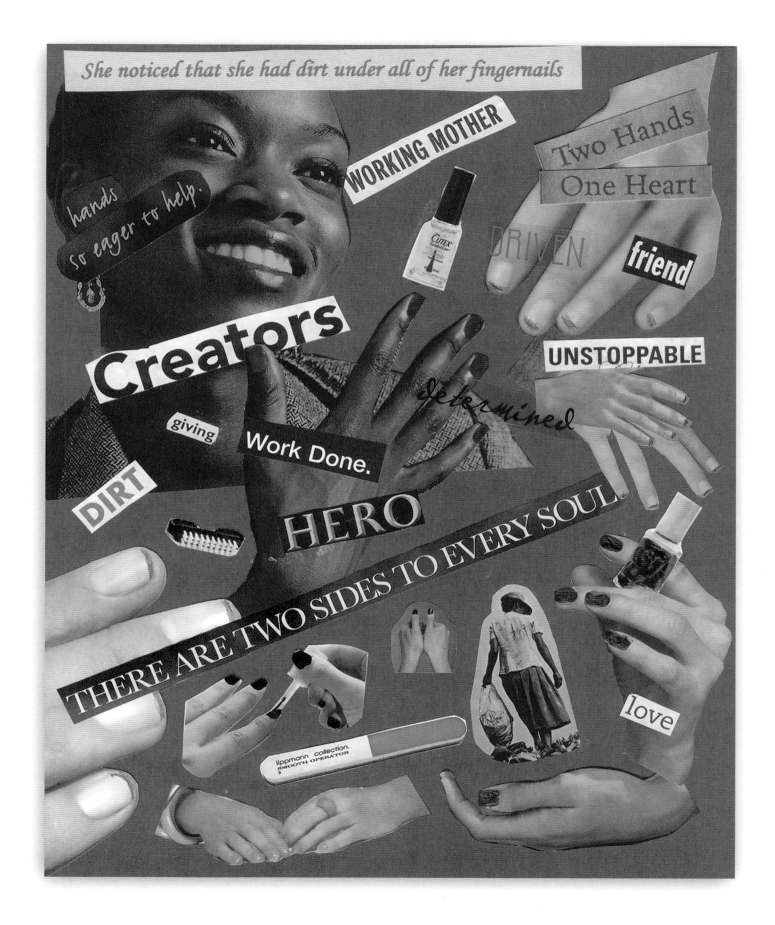

She flew...

I didn't think that there would be a statement until my phrase "She Flew..." took flight. The whole piece flew off the wall about a week into the exhibit. The glass broke. The feathers were then liberated and began to flutter in the air. The piece became animated. The phrase became illustrated. "She Flew..." became accidentally interactive.

138

Carol Chapel

In regards to the piece produced for 2005, my thoughts were focused on my sister and her 25 year marriage to her husband with mental health issues. I hope some day that she will be able to walk out the door and never look back, but she is trapped by so much around her. Effective communication seems to be almost non-existent between the two of them. Language has become a barrier or a maze she has to jump through, trying to reach a safe place with good energy and positive words. If she chooses the wrong words or the wrong day to say anything, all verbal hell breaks loose.

She never looked back...

Gale Everett Stahlke

...she never looked back

Strength

realization

She gathered up her belongings and

Why should she jump...

Roberta Smith

She whispered her sweet nothings in the puppy's ear . . .

Sarah Teutimez

She was the butterfly ...

I liked the anticipation of waiting for my phrase, seeing what could transpire after only two hours of play, and being part of a larger community project.

Laura Berman

SHE WAS SCARED… my biggest fear is having something happen to my children.

When we decided to do this project, we gathered up some craft things as well as pictures of the kids. We drove up to Julie Williams and Coleen Belisle's home to share the moment with them. Julie watched both our kids' birth, and Coleen was at our youngest daughter's birth, so we are pretty close with them.

When I got "she was scared" it was pretty easy for me to put my piece together. I ran to Kinko's and had a 3 X 11

She was scared…

panoramic shot of my son's birthday party, all lined up with kids smiling. The paper is not short on headlines that scare me… it was an easy one for me. The red words dotting the page highlight my fear of the future/politics/freaky people doing freaky things to kids.

So, that's it.

Leslie M. Wallace

Her brain storms, she thinks . . .

150

Stefanie Breder-Albright

She loved the way she felt...

My response to "She Loved the Way She Felt" was an appreciation for my Pilates instructor, Irene, who not only makes me feel good physically, but is inspiring as a teacher.

Liz Hoffman

The first *She* that popped into my mind upon reading my She Phrase, She Could Not Let It Go, was my grandmother who passed away 3 months ago at age 90. The phrase seemed to mean that I could not let my grandmother go in my memory, but also recalled how the steadfast love of my grandmother could never let her grandchildren go. My grandmother loved us grandchildren, and all people really, more totally and unconditionally than most people I have run into on the planet. She was really that kind of a pure-love-saint to me.

The way I chose to do the art was simply fun and whimsical to me. I used a picture of my grandmother's head taken in 1966, so about 40 years ago. I cut some fabric into a dress of the same comfortable style that my grandmother always wore (she cared nothing for fashion!). I have very early memories of my grandmother washing clothes in a wringer wash machine and hanging them on the line to dry. So, in the picture I had my grandmother reaching for a renegade shirt blowing off the clothesline, representing her faithful and constant love for me and the fact that we can never let each other go, no matter how far apart by distance or death the wind blows us.

She couldn't let it go . . .

Kathy Anderson

She had fire in her spirit...

Brodie Welch

She had fire in her spirit   Bodie Weld

I had once read somewhere that "art is the signature of civilizations" and I knew it to be a truth. Through art, we get a moment to look into the heart and mind of an entire world of people and places, and to see into something we have never, ourselves, known. I feel my mother embraced such a philosophy when she brought to her community *The She Project*. She allowed a community of women to sign a signature on their own stories by setting up an outlet for free impulsive expression, and to let the world in and see them exposed as the wonderfully creative force that they are.

My own piece of work was a response to my growing experiences as a young adult. Recognizing how the paths I had chosen in life were affecting me and how I tried, as I believe most people do, to hold onto that part of myself that was still innocent of the more negative experiences. I wanted to be able to express my desire to stay protected and innocent of the negative things I have lived through. Yet, as the piece progressed, I felt it began to show how I had grown to understand that staying protected can

do more harm than good. I acknowledged that I have matured into someone who can appreciate the stains that have reached my heart for they are a symbol of each choice I have made. Each path that I have traveled down is another part of a great puzzle that has created who I am today.

The phrase *She feared that the rain would stain her heart*, was a chance to explore that innocent fear in each of us of growing old, of being wounded as we try to live our lives to the fullest, and how that fear is natural. *The She Project*

She feared that the rain would stain her heart...

was a fun and eye-opening way to share that experience with other women who contributed their own signature to this community project and whom I felt a bond with because we simply shared the experience with each other. I feel that may have been my mother's intention, and I thank her for that.

Chelsea Blue Ohlgren

Each time the rain clouds form I pull out another umbrella
and hope that I can stay dry,
Stay protected
Stay innocent
stay healed.

Each time the rain drops fall I pull out another umbrella
and hope I can remain unstained.

I wonder, though... Each time I remain
Sheltered from the sky's tears
Do I learn how to shed
my own without perminent
heart break?

She Feared that the Rain would Stain Her Heart...   Blue '00

She could hardly wait.

For water, for friends, for trees, for lovers, for potential.

She waited. And she imagined: imagined this one, this person, this place, this experience, this time, would make a difference. She didn't really know what the difference would be, only that her life would become more full, more rich, more ideal, more loving, more loved.

And she waited. Waited through disappointment, through joy, through anguish, through love, through pleasure.

She could hardly wait...

She stopped waiting. And instead of waiting, she experienced the moments for which she hadn't waited: playing, family, singing, creating, laughing, running, friends. She experienced herself, the self she brought to each moment, the love that she gave to experience, to family, to friends, to lovers. She saw that it was not worth waiting. The opening love, humor, joy, and wholeness was hers to hold, hers to share.

Liz Pearce-Smith

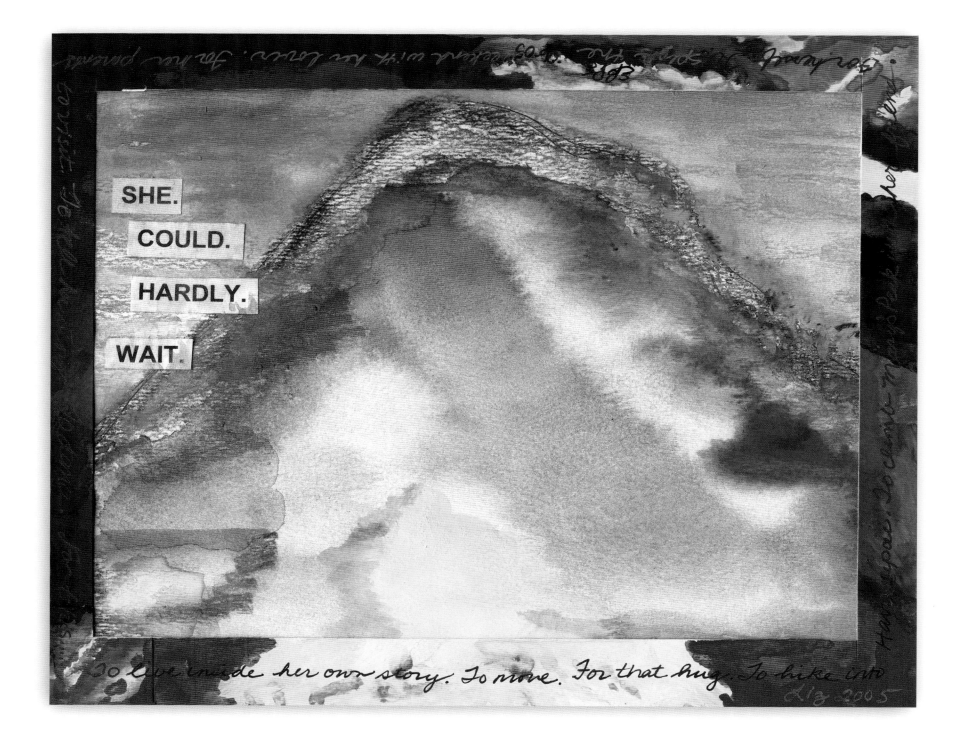

SHE.
COULD.
HARDLY.
WAIT.

When I first got my phrase, 'she was a missed opportunity,' I thought making some sort of representation was going to be difficult. After thinking about it for awhile, I started internalizing first single words, then pairings of words, and finally the whole phrase. I realized that though I often make use of small opportunities that come my way, I pretty consistently miss the big ones—even when they are simultaneously available! Or I get so wrapped up in the 'little' opportunity, that I don't even realize there was a big one. So—here I am in this piece, embracing my 'small'

She was a missed opportunity . . .

opportunity: a very pretty flower, while just around the corner/just outside my vision is the really big chance—literally the key to limitless opportunity. As often happens in my real life, I am totally oblivious, and pitifully happy with my small share. Sigh. I included some of the word pairings taken from the whole phrase: 'she was,' 'she missed,' 'missed opportunity' in the same area as my self-portrait, because they seemed to support, in the same depressing/dumb way how oblivious I can often be.

162   Joni King

She was clever, in spite of herself . . .

Sue Crawford

When I opened my phrase I was sure I could not make anything to put in my frame. I busied myself with other chores. I had waited until Sat early a.m. to open mine because I had a previous engagement Friday. The morning hours are my best. I was a little pressed because other obligations were on the calendar, starting mid-morning—so, though I had more than two hours, it was not unlimited time. And, I was sure I was supposed to work for only two hours—that was scary, too!

Eventually, after giving myself permission to not do the project, I had an idea—I pictured a woman's wind-blown flowing hair, hair flowing away from her, after her, after her thoughts, the after thoughts that she had. I wanted the hair to be filled with the thoughts and when I pondered, what are my after thoughts? What do I often rest my mind on when it is free to wander? My first action was to pull out my children's picture albums. I wanted images of the things that are often remembered, especially the ones that are dear and happy.

I wished I were more computer savvy, I would have liked to scan the precious images into her hair in a translucent way, but that was not even attempted—I imagined that taking a lifetime to learn to do, not two hours! So the colored pencils tried to guide my hand through some sketching… these were ok for me who knew what they were supposed to be, but not likely to do well for the average observer; I needed something that conveyed more of the meaning,

I felt a real obligation to limit my time to as close to 2 hours as I could, so ended up with none of my special images in the hair, instead her afterthoughts turned to cycles of life and celestial objects and beings, I ended

She had after-thoughts…

up falling back on my old friend—paper, and choosing some of my favorite papers to make a simple, pleasing image of a woman with flowing hair, and the celestial beings floating through her thoughts.

I was a little disappointed to have to leave the best thoughts out, but very much relieved just to have something to put in the frame and bring, without the shame of having failed all together.

So, I look forward to another time to try.

166

Diane Arney

Doing *The She Project* was lots of fun. My phrase was: She waited all night long. When pulling the pieces together, I thought about night and then stars and then dreaming.

I was ready for this after going to Artfest, an art retreat held last April. The person who started Artfest, Teesha Moore, gave a speech at the kick-off party about creativity and intuition. She encouraged everyone to do what they liked to do, not to judge or let other people's judgment affect them. She talked about keeping your "brain" out of your artwork, which will allow intuition and creativity to kick in and take over. She recommended playing music, so that your "brain" can't interfere.

That's what I did. After gathering stuff together for the collage, I put on music and played. The result was plenty of *She* elements—my grandmother, a printout of an e-mail about *The She Project*, a rubber stamp of a woman's torso, a stamp of a full-size woman holding a

She waited all night long...

nest (I love nests!), a self-portrait with quilt, and a photograph of me and Hannah taken by Kaiana.

Thanks for the opportunity!

Roberta Sperling

ren Ohlgren, 5/... ...070

"Judith's... ...r.net...

he Participant

She waited all night long...

and finally the dream of grandma,
Hannah, stars and Sart arrived.

We are now over 100 Women

A friend of mine tries unceasingly to lure me out of the hermit's cave of my studio. She sends me various announcements of exhibits and opportunities—from which I usually shy away. *The She Project* was different—inducing an immediate desire to be a part of this happening. It was so delightful to be working happily in my own space, and at the same time to be working within this community of women.

Since I do most of my work in Photoshop, and have a good supply of photos on file, accessing needed material for my

She took my breath....

own piece was pretty easy. Surprisingly to me, I was able to finish 10 minutes shy of two hours (my main anxiety seemed to stem from the need to stay within a time limit). Seems the spirits were with me…my particular phrase slipped easily into imagery that has been sliding through my mind for quite some time.

Diane Thies

My friends were excited about being a part of *The She Project*. I wanted so badly to be involved with the project but the thought of drawing left me way too vulnerable. Near the final hour before *The She Project*, I saw Lauren and she said to me, "I'll give you a saying, and just do anything with it so that you can be a part of the project." I thought I could at least draw a line or a circle. When I saw that my saying was 'She accepts the challenge…', I was motivated to do what I could do to accept the challenge. I am so thrilled to be a part of *The She Project*. I will never forget Lauren's gentle nudge.

She embraced the challenge…

172

Carolyn Bales

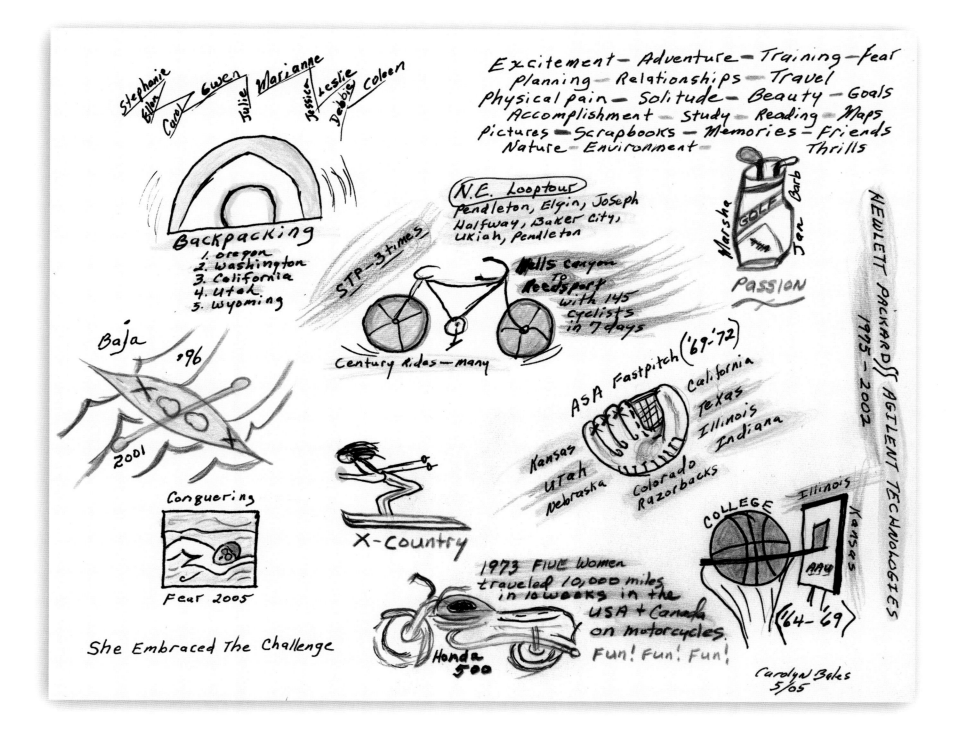

Stephanie Gwen Marianne Leslie Coleen
Ellen Carol Julie Jessica Debbie

Excitement — Adventure — Training — Fear
Planning — Relationships — Travel
Physical pain — Solitude — Beauty — Goals
Accomplishment — Study — Reading — Maps
Pictures — Scrapbooks — Memories — Friends
Nature — Environment — Thrills

Backpacking
1. Oregon
2. Washington
3. California
4. Utah
5. Wyoming

N.E. Looptour
Pendleton, Elgin, Joseph
Halfway, Baker City,
Ukiah, Pendleton

STP — 3 times

Hells Canyon to Reedsport
with 145 cyclists in 7 days

Century Rides — many

GOLF
Marsha Jon Barb
PASSION

HEWLETT PACKARD/AGILENT TECHNOLOGIES
1975 — 2002

Baja '96

2001

Conquering

Fear 2005

X-Country

ASA Fastpitch ('69-'72)
California
Texas
Illinois
Indiana
Kansas
Utah
Colorado
Nebraska Razorbacks

COLLEGE Illinois
Kansas
AAU
('64-'69)

1973 FIVE Women
traveled 10,000 miles
in 10 weeks in the
USA + Canada
on motorcycles.
Fun! Fun! Fun!

Honda 500

She Embraced The Challenge

Carolyn Bates
5/05

When I opened my *She* phrase email message, my first thought was, "What have I gotten myself into?"

I was invited to the project by my friend Liz. She said that it would be fun to play with watercolors or pen and ink. I agreed with some hesitation as I have no training, experience, or talent in art. The only drawings that I had done were the numerous assigned sketches on the subcellular details of worm innards or xylem elements in plants during my undergraduate science labs. Nonetheless, I agreed to do the project and secretly hoped that I would be able to use these subcellular images in my *She* phrase project.

I was disappointed with the phrase 'hounded by fury.' I was thwarted from using the familiar old science geek drawings. And what is fury about? My family didn't do fury; it was such an unfamiliar concept to me. And how the heck do you draw a reaction or interpretation of an emotion? I didn't want to do my project and had generated a million excuses in seconds.

Fortunately, Lauren had invited me to her '*She*-party'. Her mantra "this is not about art" and her saying "just come over and play with some materials" made me feel a bit safer about participating. Besides, I had promised that I would do a '*She*-project' and also attend the gathering. The group started with blind-contour sketches (an interesting exercise) and then women broke off into creating their own projects. I was stymied; tossing feeble attempts at my drawings and feeling a growing anxiety about creating a project in reaction to my alien phrase. All I really could do is sip on my martini and admire the creativity and abilities of the women in the room.

Fired up on gin, I soon grabbed some kind of crayons from the table and furiously scribbled out the drawing of the hound. It was kind of a joke…just a release… just trying to do something. Lauren glanced over grabbed the drawing and said "you're done!"

I was shocked and also relieved that I was done. I still protested that it wasn't 'good,' that I couldn't have something like that in the project. Lauren repeated her mantra: It's not about art. And she explained to me that the spontaneous reaction was the essence of the project. Since then I have tried to figure out what the sketch means and where it came from. Strangely, it kind of looks like my old beloved dog on a bad day. Why? I

She has been hounded by fury all her life…

don't have clear answers or perhaps do not want to look internally too deeply. The only thing that I could figure out is that I do carry anger within and perhaps some unacknowledged fury has hounded me for many years. …but, I never would have admitted it to myself or others.

Virginia Stockwell

SHE HAS BEEN
HOUNDED BY FURY
ALL OF HER LIFE...

So here I sit on a gray Thursday, moving table by table as they randomly empty and fill again and the crowded cafe´s customers dance in and out of their busy schedules for a quick cup of coffee.

I've come today to try to take them all in, or as many as I can absorb. Just black coffee for me today, no other nourishment necessary as each story feeds my spirit. Beauty before me, beauty all around.

I sit back and cherish each of these women present, represented, courageous acts of inner meaning publicly displayed. How they honor us with this sharing, baring of souls.

I delay viewing my own piece, not ready yet to see it in its place among so many other wondrous works.

"You're cheating, you're just cutting up other people's art, this isn't real art," as I worked on mine. But I was driven by a force much more powerful than those voices and couldn't stop. The process took charge and the piece emerged. Spirit directed hands and heart, where to look for what to add, guided to position one by one.

A birth of sorts.

And now, there it is. On a wall with all the other infants…microcosmic selves: some preemies, some full term, some C-sections, some natural labor, some born in joy and some in anguish. All of them alive.

All of them ours. Our voices. Our *She Project*.

She laughed so hard her belly ached…

Memories of its evening of creation already dimming, seeming tiny, inconsequential in the scope of the magnitude of this project.

I'm happily surprised to find so many collages and so much diversity. I'd had to quell nagging inner voices,

Monica Whipple

She slept soundly . . .

Jen Bouton

She loved the idea of the project, and she was delighted when she opened up her phrase; "She knew the full moon wouldn't wait…"

She sat down among friends in an apartment, kneeling by the coffee table in her own comfortable work space, colored pencils arrayed before her, and thought, I'd like to draw a woman's face. Flipping through a beautiful artbook of photography, she found a face and began to draw from it, spent a good half hour on the contours, the shape of the lips and nose, the curve of the eyes—working to shape a realistic face. Then she sat back and gazing, realized she hated it.

So she started over. Working from an intuitive pull to blue and a round, round shape of moon. She worked around the moon with flowy lines of purple and blue. Realized the moon would pop in contrast if she gave it a creamy border. Then, something in her inner world felt like tipping her head back to sing, wail, cry to the moon, or the memory and metaphor of many Moons, and a face emerged, in silhouette, with the eyes of a greek statue. She is caught in time eternally singing, calling, howling to the moon. She became a goddess of leaves and woods, with fiery red hair—a Pele, an Isis, Astarte, Demeter, Diana… And she, the artist, sat back and gazing, realized she loved it–her self portrait.

She knew the full moon couldn't wait…

180

Kirstin Schumaker

There is no way I can DO this I thought… in only TWO HOURS? Who WROTE this phrase anyway! Well, I COULD write a new one-I mean I was the one who made up this game, so, certainly I can change the rules, right?

This was to be my experience. I panicked.

My apartment was full of women who had gathered for the evening. There was an air of anticipation as one-by-one they read their phrases.

Mine was handed to me when I was ready to sit down and play. I hadn't given much thought to what I would do or to what approach I would take with my phrase. I really was playing the game the same way I figured that everyone else was.

The experience was an eye opener for me. This must be how so many other women must be feeling right now-excited, panicked, intimidated, determined. That was when I got excited. Yes, this is what the project was all about.

So I set my angst and judgment aside and started sketching. I thought about the various meanings to 'hair standing on end;' memories of old dolls with their mussed hair that could never be combed; or how the hair on our arms stands up when we're scared; or my own hair, short and spiky.

I started a blind-contour sketch of one of the women in an attempt to get focus. At one point I looked down and laughed. The sketch was surprisingly just what I

She remembered that her hair stood on end…

needed for my phrase. I was enjoying the picture, content in playing with it. I relaxed into the drawing and two hours later forced myself to just stop.

Lauren S. Ohlgren

Even in the harshest elements

life thrives,

inspiring hope and courage

in the face of doubt and uncertainty.

Finding solace

when my mind is restless or troubled,

the sanctuary of wild places

deepens my breath and

awakens my spirit.

She looked away...

I looked away,

beyond the constraints and illusions

of ordinary life,

to search and discover my own

wilderness within.

Where faith and fortitude

are born from the mystery.

Where truth and beauty are alive,

natural and free.

Cathy Bouton

BEYOND ORDINARY.

She cast away all doubt
and dreamed anyway...

186

Anna Tewes

She danced on her tippy-toes...

Tiffany Brown

She danced on her tippy-toes
   no one was watching
the same as when she exhales deep in the forest
   and no one is around to, anything
and similar to when she laughs at something to herself, out loud.

            She dances on her tippy-toes
            in spirit, through actions & reactions
            not reaching for anything

                        keep her tippy most toes on the ground.
but rather, reaching to   rooting to allow she to reach into the world
   Grounded and

                  That draws she, dancing.